This paperback edition first publish
2019 by Daisy Sailing LTD
1 Rill Farm Canteen Road
Whiteley Bank
Isle of Wight P038 3AF
www.davidrking.co.uk

ISBN 978-1-916081-51-2
This book is available at quantity discounts for bulk purchases.
For information please contact publisher or author @
daisyissailing@gmail.com

Hello You Wonderful Person

And thank you for picking up this book.

We all need something more than tea sometimes, and these quotes, sayings and poems are a reminder to feed ourselves with daily happiness, which unfortunately we tend to forget.

Simplicity is the key to consistency, and it's becoming very difficult to just be simple!

Strange we humans are: we never heed our own advice. The psychiatrist loses his mind, the hairdresser looks a mess, and the salesman can easily be sold to.

What does the writer of words do? Hopefully believes in them. The trouble is forgetfulness, or short-term memory loss, or short-term memory loss. (I blame the drugs myself).

One day, a travelling family came into town X. They found an important local man and explained that they had left the town of Y because the people there were most unfriendly and uncooperative.

'How are people in this town?' they wanted to know.

'Unfortunately,' the important man replied, shaking his head, 'they are just the way you described those in town Y.'

Upon hearing this, the family continued on their journey.

Immediately afterwards, a second travelling family arrived. They likewise found the same man, and related that they wished to settle there. They explained that they had come from the town of Y, where everyone was most friendly and cooperative. However, for reasons of the wife's health, their doctor had advised them to leave immediately. 'How are people here?' they wished to know.

Nodding his head, the local man replied, smiling: 'Just like those you described in town Y – friendly and cooperative.'

Professors of psychology say:

> ***Exposure to beauty tends to make us happier and even physically healthier, where chronic exposure to ugliness or blight has a corresponding adverse effect.***
>
> ***A Maslow.***

Sometimes we need to be told this obvious fact, for we cannot see the wood for the trees some days.

Swedish academic Hans Rosling identified a worrying trend:

Not only do many people across advanced economies have no idea that the world is becoming a much better place, but they actually even think the opposite.

This is no wonder, when the news focuses on reporting catastrophes, terrorist attacks, wars and famines.

Some clear and concise reading can be found in *The Conversation.* It's free to download to your inbox, it's produced and written by PhD academics, professors and people generally that know what they're talking about (fingers crossed) who work in many different universities in many different fields, e.g. science, business, art and culture, politics and society, health and medicine, etc.

Who wants to hear about the fact that every day some 200,000 people around the world are lifted above the US $2-a-day poverty line?

Or that more than 300,000 people get access to electricity and clean water for the first time every day?

These stories of people in low-income countries simply don't make for exciting news coverage.

- Life expectancy continues to rise.
- Child mortality continues to fall.
- Fertility rates are falling.
- Global income inequality has gone down.
- More people are living in democracies.
- Conflicts are on the decline… and on the good news goes.

Julivs Probst. Lund University.

We are surrounded by bad news every day. The journalists – the hacks – make a living selling us this negative view of the world 24/7. The soap operas are full of human misery and despair. Stop watching that rubbish. Go out into the countryside, take in a breath of air, and think how wonderful and beautiful this world really is.

Man has infinite potentiality, which, properly used, could make his life very much like his fantasies of heaven.

In potentiality, he is the most awe-inspiring phenomenon in the universe, the most creative, the most ingenious.

Throughout the ages, philosophers have sought to understand the true, the good, and the beautiful, and to speak for its forces.

Now we know that the best place to look for them is in man himself.

Abraham Maslow

There are only two things to worry about.
Either you are well, or you are sick.

If you are well,
then there is nothing to worry about.

If you are sick,
there are two things to worry about.
Either you will get well, or you will die.

If you get well,
there is nothing to worry about.

If you die,
there are two things to worry about.
Either you will go to heaven or to hell.

If you go to heaven,
there is nothing to worry about.

But if you go to hell,
you'll be so damn busy shaking hands with your friends,
you won't have time to **WORRY!**

SO WHY WORRY?

Blocks to listening

Comparing......you are remembering your story and not hearing theirs.

Mind-reading......jumping to conclusions as to outcomes, finishing sentences.

Filtering......acting on or reacting to only those pieces of information that appeal to you or you can cope with.

Judging......negative attitudes, deciding what sort of person someone is because of their appearance, etc.

Dreaming......thinking about your shopping, what happened to you or your friend, etc.

Advising......often people do not want answers to their problem until they have got it off their chest; some people never want answers.

Sparring......trying to be one up, jumping in with witty remarks, etc.

Being right......when you are sure you are right, you are not hearing the other person's points of view.

Derailing......trying to change the subject, divert their attention.

Placating......trying to make things right, soothing words, 'it will be alright in the long run', etc.

- **The most destructive habit** **Worry**
- **The greatest joy** **Giving**
- **The greatest loss** **Loss of self respect**
- **The most satisfying work** **Helping others**
- **The ugliest personality trait** **Selfishness**
- **The most endangered species** **Dedicated leaders**
- **Our greatest natural resource** **Our youth**
- **The greatest 'shot in the arm'** **Encouragement**
- **The greatest problem to overcome** **Fear**
- **The most effective sleeping pill** **Peace of mind**
- **The most crippling failure disease** **Excuses**
- **The most powerful force in life** **Love**
- **The most dangerous pariah** **A gossip**
- **The world's most incredible computer** **The brain**

- **The worst thing to be without** **Hope**
- **The deadliest weapon** **The tongue**
- **The two most power-filled words** **I can**
- **The greatest asset** **Faith**
- **The most worthless emotion** **Self-pity**
- **The most beautiful attire** **A SMILE!**
- **The most prized possession** **Integrity**
- **The most powerful channel of communication**

  Prayer
- **The most contagious spirit** **Enthusiasm**

Everyone needs this list to live by... pass it along!

Artwork D R King

All human beings belong to a single species and are descended from common stock.

They should be born equal in dignity and rights, and all form part of humanity.

What can we believe in?

Sometimes our mind tricks us. Deeds and actions speak louder than words, some say. A picture paints a thousand words, more say! But the essence in beautiful words or music also speaks volumes and reaches far more ears.

Repeating these truthful and helpful sayings will clear the mind of any misdemeanours, and pure thought will push out any discrepancies.

Save your favourites. Make some up yourself, add to or subtract from others, make it your own. Come back to it when you're feeling a little sad or down. Try to get into the habit of remembering what the words mean to you and how they make you feel.

Speak them to yourself and others whenever you can. Say them with a smile upon your face, and watch others smile too. It's good, and it feels good inside.

How can someone who can't save himself save others?

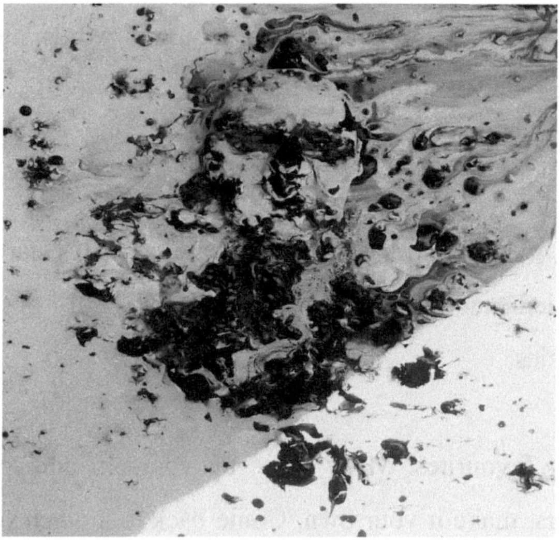

Artwork D R King

Supposing I have the key to your chains, why should your lock and my lock be the same?

What we are told affects not only our physical health but also our talents, personalities, and ability to cope

We use our tongues recklessly too often; wickedly sometimes, too. It is the best and at the same time the very worst thing in the world. We say things like 'stupid child/man/woman', 'you're thick', 'dumb', 'as daft as a brush'... And on it goes, insult after insult. They sink into our deepest being.

We need to be aware of the damage that they can do to us, and also the damage that we can do to others.

An investment in knowledge always pays the best interest

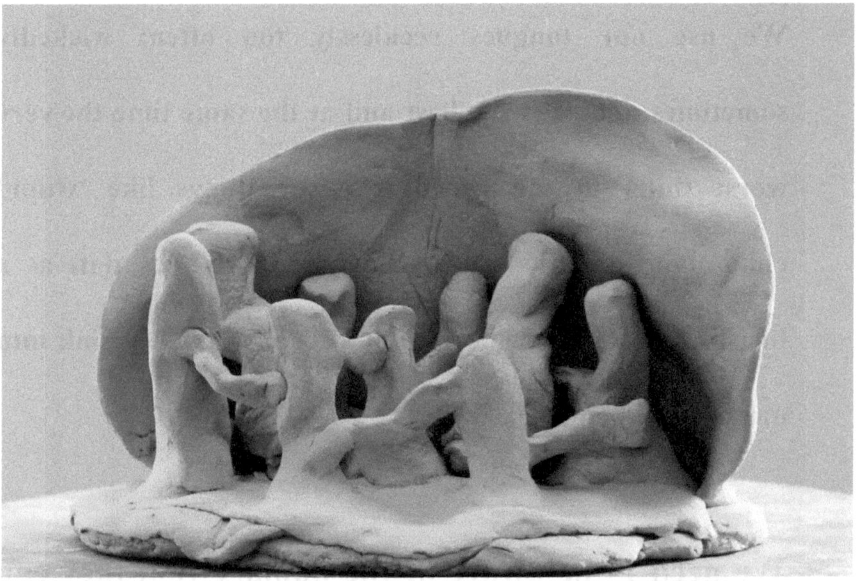

Artwork D R King

Don't begrudge spending on yourself to better your understanding of this life.
Books that teach you how to do things, or how to escape this reality. Paper qualifications to prove that you at least know a little something about a subject.

Listen to people that talk sense. Listen to your intuition, your gut feeling.

Nothing is more difficult, and therefore more precious, than to be able to decide.

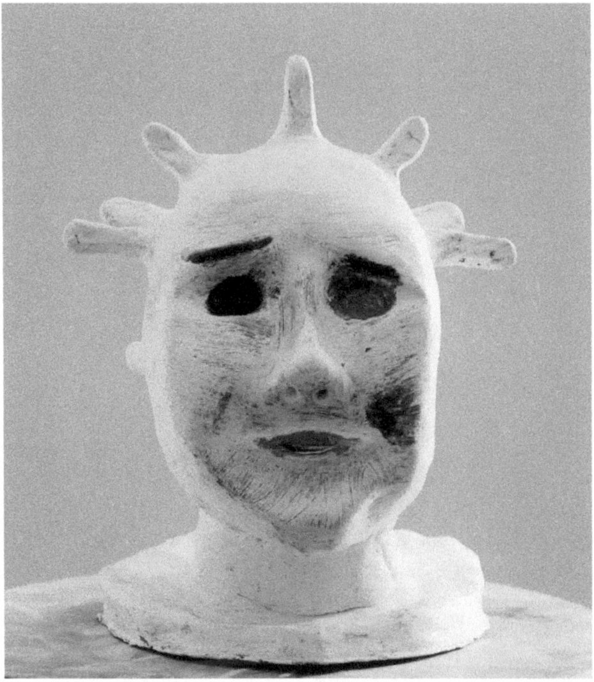

Artwork D R King

Left, right, or straight ahead, this way or that? You decide. It's so much easier if someone else has thought for you, isn't it?
But what if their advice is wrong, their direction misleading, their advice to their advantage?

You must decide. ITS OK to be wrong.

Happiness lies in being, not in having

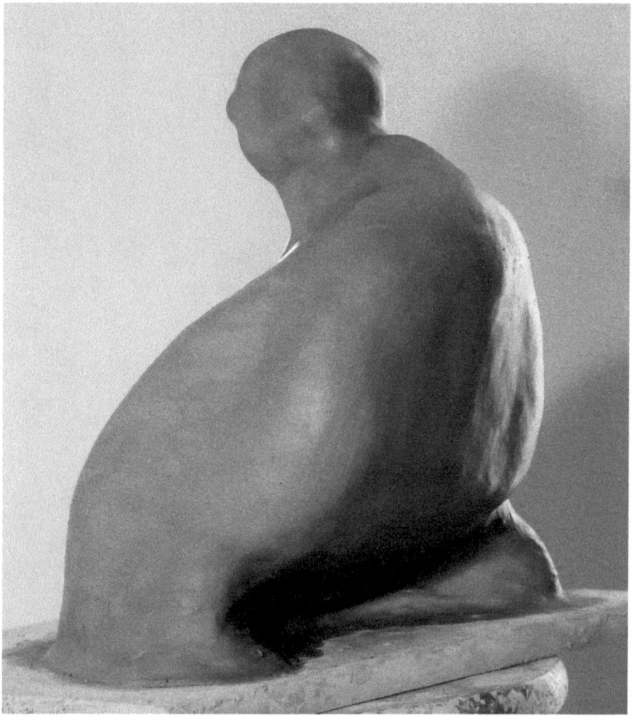

Artwork D R King

It's nice to have that new car or boat, a new pair of shoes, etc. But soon it just becomes one more thing… so many things!

You can't find happiness in things. Happiness is a by-product of something else.

The time to be happy is now. The place to be happy is here. The way to be happy is to make others so.

Happiness sometimes is:

Something to do

Someone to love

Something to hope for

Be yourself

Nothing that was real ever dies – only names, forms and illusions

Try to please all and you end up pleasing none.

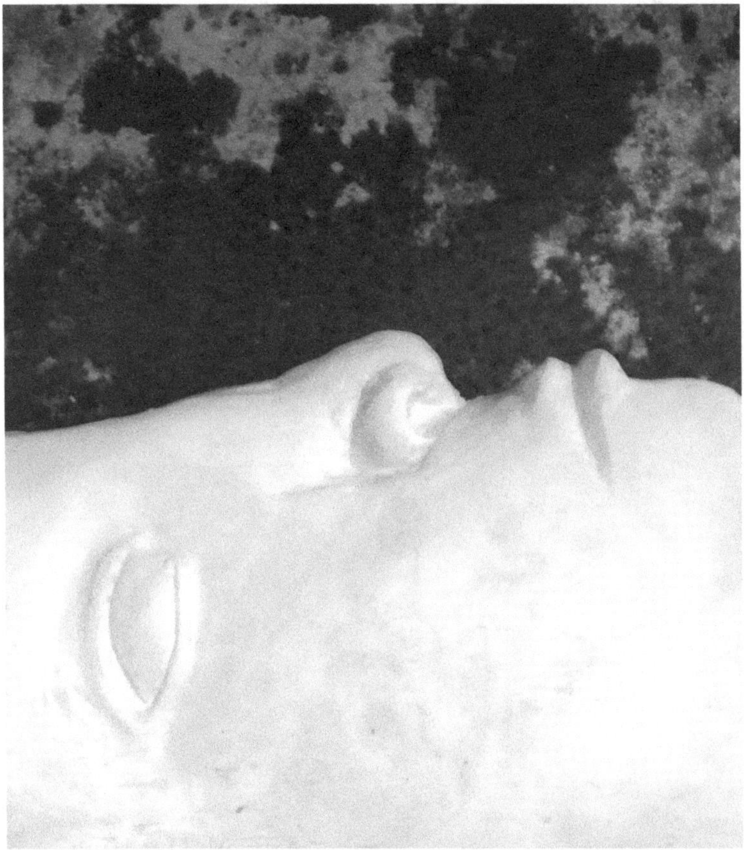

Artwork D R King

Before you speak, let your words pass through three gates:

Is it TRUE?

Is it NECESSARY?

Is it KIND?

The only time there is, is the one you are aware of

Artwork D R King

We're a long time dead. What's the point of worrying about yesterday?
How are you going to change it?

And tomorrow, can you

bring out the sunshine?

Take a deep breath NOW

ENJOY THAT BREATH

Remember it every day.

The more you look back, the less you go forward

Artwork D R King

In this age when all our lives are in front of us in a second, it can mean that we spend too much time in the past, looking at all those bloody selfies, those dogs and cats that died many moons ago.

Turn off social media for a while and think of your perfect tomorrow.

Living in the past, in our memories, is easy. It's safe, feels secure, makes us feel warm inside. That's not a bad thing on the whole, but too much thinking about the past will make you live less.

So, when you catch yourself thinking too much about those good old times (they weren't really that good, were they?)...

In Every Area Of Life, The Key Is balance

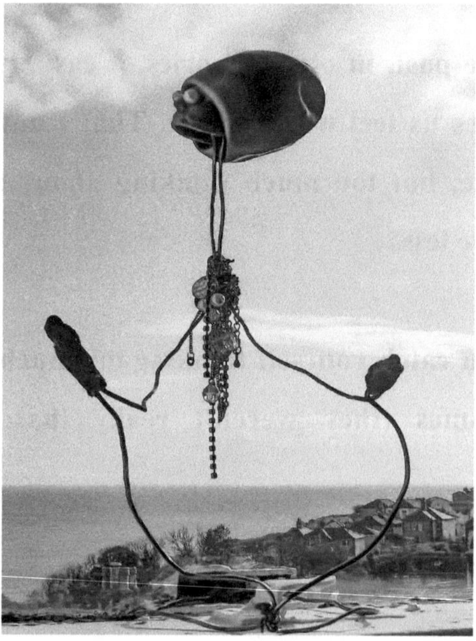

aRTWORK D R KING

- **Man sacrifices his health in order to make money.**
- **Then he sacrifices money to recuperate his health.**
- **Then he is so anxious about the future that he does not enjoy the present.**
- **The result is that he does not live in the present or the future; he lives as if he is never going to die, and then dies having never really lived.**

The Dalai Lama

The secret of success in life is to be ready for your opportunity when it comes

- The secret of success in life is known only to those who have first failed, then succeeded.

- Don’t feel envious of those that you think have everything in life.

- Being born into wealth and privilege is a burden: nothing to strive for, lack of inspiration, imagination and desire, lost with no direction, lack of values, with little understanding of the feelings for others.

- Imagine having everything you ever dreamed of, fulfilling all your fantasies. Wanting for nothing, you become nothing.

If you can't trust anyone, trust yourself

This is OK if you're feeling straight and are in control of your feelings and have no delusional thoughts – say, from too much dope, alcohol or whatever.

Or your mind might be too pickled, frayed, to think clearly. But you have to think a little bit more deeply. Why aren't you trusting anyone?

- Been lied to?
- Disrespected too much?
- Family hurt you?
- Boyfriend/girlfriend cheated on you?

On it goes. Each time one of these things happens, our trust in other humans fades.

But trust we must in others, for the sake of our own sanity and belief in all human endeavours and existence.

Keep looking. You'll find someone to trust soon. But don't trust anyone more than you can trust yourself!

Faith is the substance of things hoped for, the evidence of things not seen

- You can't really see the wind, but you know it's there because you can feel it... you can hear it... and even smell it sometimes.

- A belief in something greater than oneself – say, a better self – has got to be a positive thing.

- Faith in people and ourselves will stop us killing each other... cheating... lying... being so bloody selfish.

- Share and care a little more.

- You don't need to believe in some deity.

We are everything possible – we just don't know it yet.

Sometimes you see with your eyes, and sometimes you see with your heart

Beauty, they say, is in the eye of the beholder.

It's only skin deep. It can be manipulated – the nose made smaller, the lips more appealing, eyes wider, etc.

When you see and feel with your heart, a sensation, a tingle, happens in your body; chemicals awaken, come alight in you. It feels right, it feels OK.

Trust the heart more than the eyes sometimes.

There are only two things to aim for in life

- **First to get what you want, and after that to enjoy it.**
- **Only the wisest of humankind achieve the second.**

Those that chase money never have enough money.

Those that don't see the beauty around them never see the beauty inside another or themselves.

A smile or a good word to someone does more than all the money in the world.

The true message of success is not what you have, but what you can do without

Have a think for a minute or two! That's enough.

Remember those times when you had very little money? Wasn't life so much easier? You didn't have to think too much. Deciding what tin of baked beans you wanted: the choice was probably two. Now you probably have a dozen to choose from.

Too much choice ruins the broth. Also, when you get a bit older (like me), wearing the latest fashion craze seems a bit daft. Keep pressing that button on EBay and Amazon… that seems nuts as well.

The problem with accumulating wealth is that others want to take it from you. You don't really need three cars, six suits and thirty-two pairs of trainers, do you? (Well, maybe the trainers.)

Also, you don't need that negative person in your life running you down all the time. The racist with his limited views; the mother-in-law (fascist, but she can't help it, it's the generation). They *can* help it, and I'm not going to listen to it.

Do without it. You don't need negs in your life.

Anyone that makes you feel down, give them this book – and the time they need to change themselves.

‘Search not a wound too deep, lest thou make a new one’

Sometimes that wound doesn’t have to be a physical one; it can be a mental one as well, made worse as it keeps coming back to haunt you.

A few stitches or plaster to cover it over won’t do.

Some mental pain, such as abuse in childhood, never goes away.

We have to hide it in the back of our minds and keep it in check.

Don’t dwell on a long-ago pain. It doesn’t make it any better, only worse.

Move away from it. Tell the pain it’s over now and I’m moving on. Ta-ta, auf wiedersehen...

.

Choose a job you love, and you will never work a day in your life

It's not so much about what you do, it's who you work with that counts sometimes.

If you're one of those lucky people who know what they want to do from the day they are born, and then become it – e.g. footballer, tennis pro, pop star, etc. – then I respect and have lots of admiration for you (you lucky bastard).

But we mere mortals who are still trying to work it out – as in 'what do I do?' – must inject our humour, charisma, personalities into whatever we work in. Don't take it too seriously, and keep thinking and trying different things until one sticks and feels good.

Habit makes everything look bland – it is sleep-inducing

- **Brush your teeth from left to right or right to left**
- **Sit in a different chair**
- **Look out of the window (or not)**
- **Wear something bright, or something old (or new)**
- **Grow that beard, hair, moustache**
- **Shave or don't shave it!**

Try to think of different things to do each day, or the next day.

Sure, having a routine is good… as long as you don't get stuck in it and become rigid and fixated in your actions – and worst of all, in your thinking.

The surest way to be taken in is to think yourself craftier than other people

Oh yes, I'm smarter, prettier, a better player. Cleverer than most. I know all the answers, got the t-shirt, done it all, you can't fool me.

I don't need to listen to anyone, I'm rich and successful, a self-made man/woman.

Bang! It's over. Cancer, tumour, double-decker bus (never saw it coming), broken kerb, fallen over my self-delusion, arrogant pig-headed selfish self.

Chance and caprice rule the world

We never know sometimes when it's going to happen, that perfect moment of bliss or pain!

When a light switches on inside you, an awakening, a feeling of total euphoria.

That lucky number coming in, those things we can't explain so much in words.

That death of a friend, your death near the end, one day at a time.

We all cry and laugh for the same things

Think about it for a while.

Remember that woman or guy who looked just like someone you used to know twenty years ago – weird! Or that feeling of 'I'm sure I know her/him'.

It doesn't matter where in the world you are: when you are with others, we all share the same make-up (DNA). The only differences are those that you perceive in race, gender, clothes, environment.

Yes, all humans have unusual ways, believe in different things, eat different foods. But deep down where things really matter – where the heart aches because of grief, where smiles are wide with belief, where a loved one has passed away, the dog that was your best friend, your mum and dad gone but never forgotten – we all share this same make-up. This human existence. This human condition.

We are all part of each other. When you look at someone and for some reason you don't like them, it's something in you, not in them, that you don't like.

Change yourself and you change others.

I fear human-made hell, and I desire heaven here on earth

I've been there: hell. And I'm not going back.

The loss of a child; the loss of my best friend; the loss of my self-respect, my dignity, my courage and belief.

I'm now in heaven. I'm doing the utmost to stay here. I'm clean, drug-free, have a little wine now and then. I'm watching it, though, just in case I slip back into a nutcase.

Hell can be in the mind, and heaven can be just an illusion. You decide which.

‘Natural ability without education has more often raised a man to glory and virtue than education without natural ability’

Everyone is born with a unique set of natural abilities. If these are identified and encouraged, the individual achieves maximum satisfaction and productivity.

Abilities are not influenced by education or experience, whereas skills on the other hand are learned. A fourteen-year-old might have the natural ability to be a fine surgeon; however, he/she will not be able to perform surgery until he/she has learned the skills necessary to be a surgeon.

Skills therefore are anything a person learns through school, work, training, seminars and life.

The harder you work, the luckier you get

The more you put into something, the more you get out of it.

If you put in a little extra time, a little more of yourself, into whatever you are doing, and do it with a good heart and a smile upon your face, others will notice that they feel good around you. Then all manner of things might happen: an invitation out somewhere; more money in your wage packet; a different job offer; romance.

Good fortune will follow you and be with you. It’s not luck, really: it’s you.

I am only one, but still I am one

I cannot do everything, but still I can do something. I will not refuse to do something I can do.

We can all do something, if we don't fill our minds with too many things – all the distractions that we put in place to stop ourselves doing something! (Why do we do that?) Just smiling at that stranger in the street is doing something, something good, something nice, for someone else.

When you start doing something, it's amazing what you can actually do.

Think it, repeat it over to yourself a few times, imagine it, and in time you might become it.

If you don’t stand for something, you’ll fall for anything

Have some kind of a view on things. Research it and know what you are taking about – that always helps!

What makes you smile? Find out.

Have a belief, a faith in yourself first.

Beware the trickster, the person who tells you what you want to hear, trying to fool you and persuade you into their way of thinking.

Let deeds match words

I'll pick you up tomorrow 10 a.m. OK! I promise I will be there.

I could write a book. I could ride a horse. Anyone can do that, can't they? Why should I bother doing something when I already know I can do it?

Stop it, you're smoking too much. The proof is in the pudding. You have to work at that recipe. Read the instructions, use your hands, think about it.

- ***Showing is better than talking. Too much instruction is worse than none.***

- ***Do something good and don't tell anyone about it.***

I walk firmer and more securely uphill than down

When we start to get going on life's journey, one rung of the ladder at a time – learning a little about ourselves and others, learning what we are inside, and striving to better ourselves not necessarily for money, fame or fortune, but for our soul's sake – we slowly (or some of us too quickly) start to climb that hill. Maybe it's called success, ego, etc- and everybody pats us on the back: they are all our friends when we start to climb!

But as soon as something goes wrong and we think we're reaching the top, then we topple over and start the descent.

- **Where are those friends now?**
- **Where are those people that supposedly were by my side?**
- **They've gone on to the next one who's climbing the hill.**

'Oh God, that men should put an enemy in their mouths to steal away their brains!'

Don't we just know it? Think before you speak.

I haven't done much thinking in my life. My mouth has got me into endless disputes, troubles, beatings and even prison.

I guess my thinking must have been so pickled, my ego so out of control, I lost all reason.

Anyway, enough about me!

Curb it. Remember, that tongue can be the best of things – or the worst.

Don’t judge those that try and fail, judge only those that fail to try

Over 200 jobs, sacked numerous times. ‘Sorry Dave’ we’re going to have to let you go. You can’t possibly do that; you’re not qualified enough; you don’t know enough; you haven’t got enough experience; you’re not fast enough.

So many doubters out there, all stuck in one lane, each stuck behind the next doubter.

Never give up. Never give up believing in You.

The person who asks a question is a fool for a minute; the person who does not ask is a fool for life.

- Keep asking. Keep asking 'WHY' all the time. Don't let that word escape you.
- 'Why? Because when we stop asking ourselves 'Why', We stop living inside, we're dead to the world, we're dead to **ourselves**.
- Why' keeps us waking up in the morning.

'Art is born of the observation and investigation of nature'

- Art is along a bit, down a bit, from your nose.
- It's out of your window, it's in the trees!
- It's everything inside you and outside you, you've just got to listen to it.
- Hear the songs of the birds.
- Feel the wind on your face.
- Take an unknown step.
- Think a different thought.
- Experience something that you haven't experienced before.
- Take a breath and hold it as long as you can.
- Freedom is art.
- Art is freedom.

Don't Let The Paranoia Destroy Yeh!

ArTWork d r king

Sometimes a sound appears...

Body jumps by itself, ears strain towards the noise, you feel sick, a hollow dreaded sensation in the pit of your stomach.

The TV crackles its electrifying power, directly linking your already overworking, raging brain, electrical sensors binding, fusing us together.

A thought appears! Disappears?

A sign, this time on the wall. Heart races, calm down, calm down, no one is there.

It's the fact there's no one there that's the trouble!

If I am to die this time... at least let it not be alone!

My mind's doors are open now, thousands of thoughts mingling, crossing over each other, being torn by ripped streams of consciousness.

'Fuck!' Paranoia again.

Better a shorter happy life

than a long and miserable one.

Better a smile upon the face

than a long one.

Better a good word for someone

than an unkind one.

Better to be true to oneself,

and live a life well, with no regrets,

blame or sorrow,

thinking of now and never tomorrow.

For when the last breath leaves,

and the wind calms down,

the tune of life

still goes around.

What do you believe about yourself?

Do you see yourself as a strong and capable person who will succeed in attaining the vision you hold for yourself? Or do you see yourself as ineffective and overwhelmed? Either way, you'll be right.

Your beliefs will dictate the circumstances in your life – your reality.

Much as an electrician rewires circuits in a faulty electrical system, if we want to succeed and achieve our highest potential, we must replace any negative beliefs we hold about ourselves with positive ones.

Once attained, that foundation of powerful beliefs will help us on our path to success and fulfilment!

- **Your potential is unlimited.**
- **Aspire to a high place.**
- **Believe in your abilities, your tastes, your judgement.**
- **Imagine and perceive that wish as reality.**
- **Back up your image with enthusiasm and courage.**

Feel the reality of your 'new' self. Live in the expectation of greater things, and your subconscious will actualise them.

Deep within you dwells your VISION...

...It's you in the form of your purest potential: your real self.

Your true vision is your core being telling you who you really are. It defines your personal greatness.

To see your vision and mould it into a recognisable thought form, you must sweep aside old, limited beliefs about who you thought you were, and see your true self – the self who is made from innate wisdom, power and intelligence. That self can reach for your highest potential and establish a life built on clear purpose.

Once your vision is clear to you, you may not know how to accomplish it. Few of us do. But just as a seed planted in warm earth and sunlight knows exactly how to grow into a plant, your vision has within it the cosmic wisdom to bring itself to fruition. In order to germinate, you need only to listen to your inner guidance. Act upon what it tells you. Take one step, then the next. Just as attention from sunlight and rain nourishes the seed into a strong, healthy plant, the more energy you shower onto your vision, the more it will grow.

You'll be guided automatically to the right people, places and situations to move you ahead on your journey.

The vision growing within you is the unlimited you, the powerful you, the wise you.

It's the you who has the confidence to step forward with passion and reach for the most challenging opportunities.

Toni Turner

Until one is committed

There is hesitance, the chance to draw back, always ineffectiveness.

Concerning all acts of initiative (and creation), there is one elementary truth, the ignorance of which kills the countless ideas and splendid plans; the moment one definitely commits oneself, then providence moves too.

.

A whole stream of events issues from the decision, raising in one's favour all manner of unforeseen incidents and meetings and material assistance, which no one could have dreamed would come their way.

William Hutchison Murray.

Thoughts: mind over matter

Your every thought produces a biochemical reaction in the brain. The brain then releases chemical signals that are transmitted to the body, where they act as the messengers of the thought.

The thoughts that produce the chemicals in the brain allow your body to feel exactly the way you were just thinking. So, every thought produces a chemical that is matched by a feeling in your body.

Essentially, when you think happy, inspiring or positive thoughts, your brain manufacturers chemicals that make you feel joyful, inspired or uplifted.

For example, when you appreciate an experience that is pleasurable, the brain immediately makes a neurotransmitter called dopamine, which turns the brain and body on in appreciation of that experience and causes you to begin to feel excited.

If you have hateful, angry or self-deprecating thoughts, the brain also produces chemicals called neuropeptides that the body responds to in a comparable way. You feel hateful, angry or unworthy.

You see, your thoughts immediately do become matter. When the body responds to a thought by having a feeling, this initiates a response in the brain. The brain, which constantly monitors and evaluates the status of the body, notices that the body is feeling a certain way. In response to that body feeling, the brain generates thoughts that produce corresponding chemical messengers: you begin to think the way you are feeling. Thinking creates feeling, and then feeling creates thinking, in a continuous circle.

This loop eventually creates a particular state in the body that determines the general nature of how we feel and behave. We will call this a state of being. For example, suppose a person lives most of her life in a repeating circle of thoughts and feelings related to insecurity. The moment she has a thought about not being good enough or smart enough or enough of anything, her brain releases chemicals that produce a feeling of insecurity.

Now she is feeling the way she was just thinking. Once she is feeling insecure, she then will begin to think the way she was just feeling. In other words, her body is now causing her to think. This thought leads to more feelings of insecurity, and so the cycle perpetuates itself. If this person's thoughts and feelings continue, year after year, to generate the same biological feedback loop between her brain and her body, she will exist in a state of being that is called insecure.

The more we think the same thoughts, which then produce the same chemicals, which cause the body to have the same feelings, the more we physically become modified by our thoughts. In this way, depending on what we are thinking and feeling, we create our state of being. What we think about and the energy or intensity of these thoughts directly influences our health, the choices we make, and ultimately the quality of our life.

Dr Joe Dispenza

How to keep your head when all around are losing theirs

Anxiety.

Causes constantly raised levels of the stress hormone cortisol. Prolonged exposure to cortisol raises the risk of developing depression. One key to fending off anxiety is to develop resilience skills.

Get physical.

If you feel yourself physically contracting – a bad case of social panic. Try mind/body methods to help you to cope. Techniques such as meditation, deep breathing, yoga or exercise can be used to calm the body, so the fight-or-flight response will switch off sooner.

Stay curious.

In times of stress it can feel instinctively right to hunker down and resist risky changes. The opposite works best. Highly resilient people continually learn new ways of doing things and frequently change how they interact with their circumstances. The least resilient people drift into a tightening-up condition where they try to avoid change and new experiences.

Keep a gratitude journal.

Keeping a record of the things in your day that bring joy and gratitude can prove an effective way to break the worried brain's habit of fixating only on stress-induced things that have gone wrong or which might go awry.

Build your community.

The more you are part of the community, the more you will have higher levels of resilience against life's knocks. Joining clubs, associations, anything where there is a spirit of people will help you.

A Rolling Stone

There's sunshine in the heart of me,
My blood sings in the breeze;
The mountains are a part of me,
I'm fellow to the trees.
My golden youth I'm squandering,
Sun-libertine am I;
A-wandering, a-wandering.
Until the day I die.

I was once, I declare, a Stone-Age man,
And I roomed in the cool of a cave;
I have known, I will swear, in a new life-span,
The fret and the sweat of a slave:
For far over all that folks hold worth,
There lives and there leaps in me
A love of the lowly things of earth,
And a passion to be free.

To pitch my tent with no prosy plan,

To range and to change at will;
To mock at the mastership of man,
To seek Adventure's thrill.
Carefree to be, as a bird that sings;
To go my own sweet way;
To reck not at all what may befall,
But to live and to love each day.

To make my body a temple pure
Wherein I dwell serene;
To care for the things that shall endure,
The simple, sweet and clean.
To oust out envy and hate and rage,
To breathe with no alarm;
For Nature shall be my anchorage,
And none shall do me harm.

To shun all lures that debauch the soul,
The orgied rites of the rich;
To eat my crust as a rover must
With the roughneck down in the ditch.

To trudge by his side whate'er betide;
To share his fire at night;
To call him friend to the long trail-end,
And to read his heart aright.

To scorn all strife, and to view all life,
With the curious eyes of a child;
From the plangent sea to the prairie,
From the slum to the heart of the Wild.
From the red-rimmed star to the speck of sand,
From the vast to the greatly small;
For I know that the whole for good is planned,
And I want to see it all.

To see it all, the wide world-way,
From the fig-leaf belt to the Pole;
With never a one to say me nay,
And none to cramp my soul.
In belly-pinch I will pay the price,
But God! let me be free;
For once I know in the long ago,

They made a slave of me.

In a flannel shirt from earth's clean dirt,
Here, pal, is my calloused hand!
Oh, I love each day as a rover may,
Nor seek to understand.
To ENJOY is good enough for me;
The gipsy of God am I;
Then here's a hail to each flaring dawn!
And here's a cheer to the night that's gone!
And may I go a-roaming on
Until the day I die!
Then every star shall sing to me
Its song of liberty;
And every morn shall bring to me
Its mandate to be free.
In every throbbing vein of me
I'll feel the vast Earth-call;
O body, heart and brain of me
I am in part All.

by Robert W. Service

The Men That Don't Fit In
by Robert W. Service

There's a race of men that don't fit in,
A race that can't stay still;
So, they break the hearts of kith and kin,
And they roam the world at will.
They range the field and rove the flood,
And they climb the mountain's crest;
Theirs is the curse of the gypsy blood,
And they don't know how to rest.

If they just went straight they might go far;
They are strong and brave and true;
But they're always tired of the things that are,
And they want the strange and new.
They say: 'If I find my proper groove,
What a deep mark I would make!'
So they chop and change, and each fresh move
Is only a fresh mistake.

And each forgets, as he strips and runs
With a brilliant, fitful pace,
It's the steady, quiet, plodding ones
Who win in the lifelong race.
And each forgets that his youth has fled,
Forgets his prime is past,
Till he stands one day, with a hope that's dead,
In the glare of the truth at last.

He has failed, he has failed; he has missed his chance;
He has just done things by half.
Life's been a jolly good joke on him,
And now is the time to laugh.
Ha, ha! He is one of the Legion Lost;
He was never meant to win;
He's a rolling stone, and it's bred in the bone;
He's a man who won't fit in.

Look Closer, See ME

What do you see, nurse? What do you see?
What are you thinking when you're looking at me?

A crabbed old woman, not very wise,
Uncertain of habit, with faraway eyes,

Who dribbles her food and makes no reply
When you say in a loud voice, 'I do wish you'd try!'

Who seems not to notice the things that you do,
And forever is losing a stocking or shoe?

Who, resisting or not, lets you do as you will
With bathing and feeding, the long day to fill.

Is that what you're thinking? Is that what you see?
Then open your eyes, nurse, you're not looking at ME.

I'll tell you who I am as I sit here so still, As I do your bidding, as I eat at your will.

I'm a small child of ten, with a Mother and Father, Brothers and sisters who love one another.

A young girl of sixteen, with wings on her feet,
Dreaming that soon a lover she'll meet.

A bride soon at twenty, my heart gives a leap Remembering the vows we have promised to keep.

At twenty-five now, I have young of my own
Who need me to guide them, and a secure and happy home.

A woman of thirty, my young they grow fast,
Bound to each other with ties that should last.

At forty, my young sons have grown and have gone,
But my man's beside me to see I don't mourn.

At fifty, once more babies play round my knee.

Again, we know children, my husband and me.
Dark days are upon me, my husband is dead.
I look to the future and shudder with dread.
For my young are all busy rearing young of their own,
And I think of the years and the love I have known.

I'm an old woman now, and nature is cruel.
'Tis her jest to make old age look like a fool.

The body, it crumbles, grace and vigour depart,
There is now a stone, where I once had a heart.

But inside this old carcass, a young girl still dwells,
And now and again my battered heart swells.

I remember the joys, I remember the pain,
And I'm living and loving all over again.
I think of the years, all too few, gone too fast,
And accept the stark fact that nothing can last.
So, open your eyes, people, open and see,
Not a crabbed old woman. Look closer. See ME.
Phyllis McCormack

There's an elephant in the room
By Terry Kettering

There's an elephant in the room.
It is large and squatting,
So it's hard to get around it.
Yet we squeeze by with 'How are you?' and 'I'm fine.' And a thousand other forms of trivial chatter.

We talk about the weather.
We talk about work.
We talk about everything – except the elephant in the room.

There's an elephant in the room.
We all know it is there.
We are thinking about the elephant as we talk together.
It is constantly on our minds.

For you see, it is a very big elephant.
It has hurt us all.
But we do not talk about the elephant in the room.

Oh, please say her name,
Oh, please say 'Barbara' again.
Oh, please let's talk about the elephant in the room.
For if we talk about her death,
Perhaps we can talk about her life?

Can I say 'Barbara' to you and not have you look away?

For if I cannot, you are leaving me alone

In a room – with an elephant.

Please Hear What I'm Not Saying

Don't be fooled by me.
Don't be fooled by the face I wear
for I wear a mask, a thousand masks,
masks that I'm afraid to take off,
and none of them is me.

Pretending is an art that's second nature with me,
but don't be fooled,
for God's sake don't be fooled.
I give you the impression that I'm secure,
that all is sunny and unruffled with me, within as well as without,
that confidence is my name and coolness my game,
that the water's calm and I'm in command
and that I need no one,
but don't believe me.
My surface may seem smooth but my surface is my mask,
ever-varying and ever-concealing.
Beneath lies no complacence.

Beneath lies confusion, and fear, and aloneness.
But I hide this. I don't want anybody to know it.
I panic at the thought of my weakness exposed.
That's why I frantically create a mask to hide behind,
a nonchalant sophisticated facade,
to help me pretend,
to shield me from the glance that knows.

But such a glance is precisely my salvation, my only hope,
and I know it.
That is, if it's followed by acceptance,
if it's followed by love.
It's the only thing that can liberate me from myself,
from my own self-built prison walls,
from the barriers I so painstakingly erect.
It's the only thing that will assure me
of what I can't assure myself,
that I'm really worth something.
But I don't tell you this. I don't dare to, I'm afraid to.
I'm afraid your glance will not be followed by acceptance,

will not be followed by love.
I'm afraid you'll think less of me,
that you'll laugh, and your laugh would kill me.
I'm afraid that deep-down I'm nothing
and that you will see this and reject me.

So I play my game, my desperate pretending game,
with a facade of assurance without
and a trembling child within.
So begins the glittering but empty parade of masks,
and my life becomes a front.
I idly chatter to you in the suave tones of surface talk.
I tell you everything that's really nothing,
and nothing of what's everything,
of what's crying within me.
So when I'm going through my routine
do not be fooled by what I'm saying.
Please listen carefully and try to hear what I'm not saying,
what I'd like to be able to say,
what for survival I need to say,
but what I can't say.

I don't like hiding.
I don't like playing superficial phony games.
I want to stop playing them.
I want to be genuine and spontaneous and me
but you've got to help me.
You've got to hold out your hand
even when that's the last thing I seem to want.
Only you can wipe away from my eyes
the blank stare of the breathing dead.
Only you can call me into aliveness.
Each time you're kind, and gentle, and encouraging,
each time you try to understand because you really care,
my heart begins to grow wings--
very small wings,
very feeble wings,
but wings!

With your power to touch me into feeling
you can breathe life into me.
I want you to know that.

I want you to know how important you are to me,
how you can be a creator--an honest-to-God creator--
of the person that is me
if you choose to.
You alone can break down the wall behind which I
tremble,
you alone can remove my mask,
you alone can release me from my shadow-world of
panic,
from my lonely prison,
if you choose to.
Please choose to.

Do not pass me by.
It will not be easy for you.
A long conviction of worthlessness builds strong walls.
The nearer you approach to me the blinder I may strike
back.
It's irrational, but despite what the books say about man
often I am irrational.
I fight against the very thing I cry out for.

But I am told that love is stronger than strong walls
and in this lies my hope.
Please try to beat down those walls
with firm hands but with gentle hands
for a child is very sensitive.

Who am I, you may wonder?

I am someone you know very well.

For I am every man you meet

and I am every woman you meet.

With kind permission from Charles C. Finn.

'The true measure of a man is how he treats someone who can do him absolutely no good'

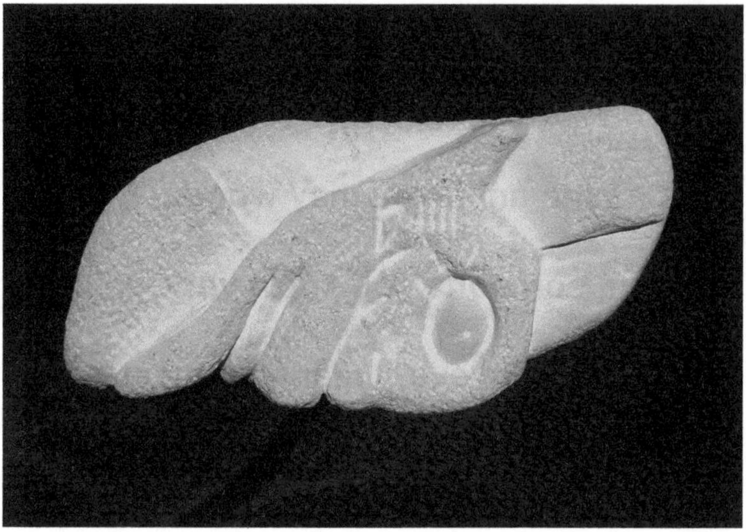

Artwork D R King

The schizophrenic, the loner, the misunderstood, and others.

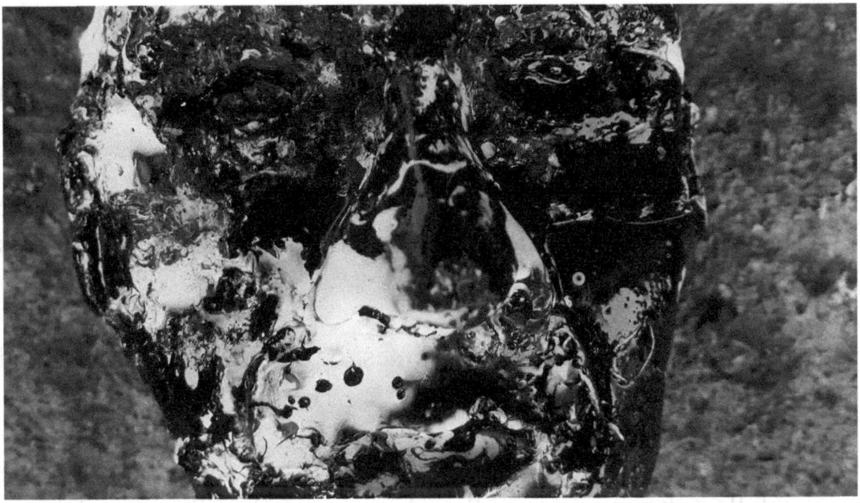

Artwork d r king

The schizophrenic ceases to be schizophrenic when he meets someone by whom he feels understood.

Who cannot do as he desires
Must do what lies within his power
Folly is to wish for
what cannot be

The wise man holds that from such wishing he must free himself.

Our joy and grief consist alike in this.

In knowing what to dream and what to do. Sometimes is it not always good to have one's wish.

What once seemed sweet often turns bitter. People's tears have been shed a thousand times at having lived out one's fantasies and desires.

Therefore, O reader of these lines, be good to others and good will come to you.

The acquisition of any knowledge is always of use to the intellect; because it may thus drive out useless things and retain the good.

Know that all things work together for good, to them that love.

Leonardo da Vinci.

We are each born into our own unique situation.

ArtWork. D. R. king

We obsess about death, so why don't we think more about being born?

All human beings begin life being born – and all human beings die. In these two ways, we are finite: our lives are not endless, but they begin, and they come to an end. Historically, however, philosophers have concentrated attention on only one of these two ways in which we are finite: mortality.

Philosophers have said little about being born and how it shapes our existence. An exception is some recent work in feminist philosophy, for instance by Luce Irigaray and Adriana Cavarero – but even here, being born has been overshadowed by giving birth and motherhood.

So how does being born organise human existence? First, let's clarify that for human beings, to be born is to begin to exist at a certain point in time, and to do so being conceived and gestated in and then exiting from

the womb – historically the maternal womb, although transgender pregnancies are changing this. We thereby come into the world with a specific body, and in a given place, set of relationships and situation in society, culture, and history.
Because of this helplessness of human babies and infants – and children's prolonged need for nurturing and education – we begin life utterly dependent on the people who care for us physically and emotionally. Often, we become more independent over time, but never completely or permanently so. We all remain dependent on others – in respect of our means of subsistence, language, emotional well-being and basic social trust. Once we remember that we begin life as babies and infants, dependency emerges as more basic than independence – independence takes place against a background of dependence, not vice versa.

Because of our initial dependency, our early relationships with our caregivers have huge formative effects on us. They form ourselves: our patterns of emotional reaction, dispositions, habits and traits – and the personalities into which they are organised. None of this is set in stone – we can, of course, be deeply affected and reformed by subsequent relationships. But we are open to new relationships in ways shaped by the previous ones. When we consider birth, then, we see that relationships with others make us the individuals we are – our individual selfhood arises within a background of relationships.

Me, myself and I

At birth, each individual comes into a unique situation in the world, made up of a unique combination of historical, social, ethnic, geographical, familial and generational circumstances. One's initial natal situation affects every subsequent life situation one comes to be in – including by affecting whatever choices one makes in response to these situations. All of one's successive situations flow down through one's life, however indirectly, from one's birth.

We are each born into our own unique situation.

Our natal situations are given to us, not chosen – and as soon as we are born we begin to imbibe the culture around us. So, first and foremost, we are inheritors and receivers of culture and history. We may develop capacities to question, criticise and change what we have received, but this happens on the prior basis of reception.

Why have I been leading the particular life I have since birth? I may wonder 'Why am I me?' or 'Why is this the life I'm leading and none other?' Eastern and Western religious traditions offer various answers – for example, by referring to our immortal souls as in Christianity, or cycles of rebirth, as in Hinduism. But perhaps, my being born me is a fact that cannot be explained, only accepted.

We can explain, at least to a point, why the particular body that I happen to be born with was conceived (my parents met, a particular sperm fertilised a particular egg on a given occasion – and the rest). But that does not explain why this body is the one whose life I happen to be leading and experiencing directly from the inside.

This is just a fact, and because it is inexplicable, a dimension of mystery pervades my existence. That mystery can generate anxiety – one of several forms of birth anxiety. Philosophers (Heidegger, for example) have said much about anxiety about death, but being born also presents anxieties and existential difficulties.

Early days

It can seem perplexing that I ever arrived in existence having not previously been there. And it can be troubling that we cannot remember being born, or indeed remember early childhood – the phenomenon known as 'infantile amnesia'.

This amnesia is a consequence of the staged development of the memory and cognitive systems during childhood. As we rise to more advanced forms of memory, we lose access to earlier memories laid down in less advanced forms. In turn, our staged cognitive development is a consequence of birth: we are born very immature and unformed but develop, eventually, to reach high levels of cognitive sophistication.

Yet the early years that we forget are the most formative for us. We therefore end up with much of our emotional lives and reactions as mysteries to us. Why do we fall in and out of love with the people we do? Why does this song move me to tears and leave you cold? Infantile amnesia leaves us strangers to ourselves in important respects – and this is disconcerting.

These are just some features of human existence which are thrown into relief once we remember that we are not only mortal, but also natal. Being born is a fundamental, not a trivial or accidental, feature of human life – and human existence overall has the shape it does because we are born.

by Alison Stone, Lancaster University

Creating a password

cabbage

sorry the password must be more than 8 characters

boiled cabbage

sorry the password must contain 1 numerical number

1 boiled cabbage

sorry the password cannot have any blank spaces

50fuckingboiledcabbages

sorry the password must contain at least 1 uppercase character

50FUCKINGboiledcabbages

sorry the password cannot use more than one uppercase character consecutively

50FuckingBoiledCabbagesShovedUpYourArseIfYouDon'tGiveMeAccessImmediately

sorry that password is already in use.

It's getting worse in the land of:
intermindnumingnet, don't lose it, smile at the madness of it?

Out of confusion comes clarity

Turn off all notifications on your Android or iPhone **NOW**. Nothing is more important than yourself. Not little Henry, Megan or Elizabeth or that lovely wife of yours (unless they're drowning).

If you don't look after your own sanity, how can you be of any help to anybody? Part from others whose sanity is questionable. Stop conversing with them.

Email-Facebook-Instagram-Snapchat-WhatsApp-allthatcrap...
CAN wait.

Let your mind work out what it needs to work out by itself (in sleep is best), with no outside interference. Close your eyes for a while, take a few deep breaths, listen to your heartbeat, and feel glad and relieved that you can.

Life has no meaning: it's YOU who brings meaning to it.

Oh, what's the meaning of life? 'What's it all about, Alfie?'(Cilla Black)

We've been shouting and screaming and thinking about this for thousands of years. Oh God, why am I so susceptible to others opinions? I don't know what's true any more.

There is no meaning of life: you're the meaning. Just be **YOU**; just be content with **YOUR** own being. **Sometimes the more you seek, the less you find.**

Pop outside into the countryside, or just look outside your window. Listen – not to the hustle and bustle of things, but to the birds singing, the wind blowing in the trees.

Look at the natural smiles on babies faces, kids playing simple made-up games. What's that telling you? Smile at someone – some of them actually smile back! That's one of the things **YOU** can do to bring meaning to life.

I don't really care whether my glass is half full or half empty. I'm just happy to have a glass.

Try thinking a little more about others. I know it's hard, but please, once or twice a day. Try not to think too much about your own predicaments, problems etc. Spend a bit more time thinking about those that are near to you, and those that are dear to you. Be grateful and appreciate what you have. Think for a moment of those that have nothing: no love in their lives, no happiness in their hearts, no hope, no country, no home to go back to.

Feel humble sometimes and that emotion can change the world.

artwork d r king

What is the purpose of life?

If you thought you had found the answer to that question, wouldn't it make your life purposeless?

How happy can you be? How happy can you make others? What is going to happen tomorrow, next week, next year? Good health one day, bad the next. Everything's hunky-dory, life's great now, so live it **NOW** – for none of us knows what's in store for us. Strive every day to improve your human nature. Find your purpose, and wish good health and fortune to all those who occupy this world now.

There are no enlightened people, only enlightened actions

Actions speak louder than words. How many times have we heard this?

OK, maybe there are some enlightened people (ME ME ME, it's all about ME! Sorry about that.) Muhammad, Jesus Christ, the Buddha, the Dalai Lama, he seems a nice guy.

But on the whole, beware of anyone who tells you they are enlightened. They're probably a little touched. Humour them, and say 'Of course you are. What are your deeds? What have you done for the earth?'

Doing something good for someone else and not telling anyone: now that's a start to enlightenment.

Experience has taught me that those who matter don’t mind, and those who mind don’t matter

Mind you, that’s not an excuse to act like a fool and do whatever you want, is it? (Sorry mum, dad, uncles and aunties, friends, cats and dogs and anyone else I’ve upset.)

If you go around in life trying to please everybody, you end up pleasing… NO ONE.

Give and take is a sound policy in most things.

The great man is the one who does not lose his child-heart, the original good heart with which every man is born.

Mencius

Unfortunately, or fortunately, when we start to grow, our environment, parents and genes will dictate to a certain degree how we turn out. We can't choose our parents, can we? We didn't get a say in how they brought us up when we were young. We have to try to figure this life out by ourselves sometimes. Or, if we are lucky, we will find somebody who can guide us a little to our true good-nature selves.

Want to be happier? Try getting to know yourself better

If you develop an awareness of how you feel, you are more likely to be able to change negative thinking patterns.

The unexamined life is not worth living, said the Greek philosopher Socrates. He was reflecting on the expression 'Know Thyself' – an aphorism inscribed on the temple of Apollo at Delphi, and one of the ultimate achievements in ancient Greece.

While we walk around the world more or less successful in our endeavours, many of us sometimes have the nagging feeling that we don't truly know ourselves. Why do we really feel and behave the way we do? While we have some ideas about who we are, our understanding of ourselves is often patchy and inconsistent. So, is self-knowledge something we should strive for, or are we better off living in blissful ignorance? Let's examine the research.

By self-knowledge, psychologists mean having an understanding of our feelings, motivations, thinking patterns and tendencies. These give us a stable sense of self-worth and a secure grip on our values and motivations. Without self-knowledge we cannot have an internal measure of our own worth.

It is an advantage to learn how to recognise our feelings. The experience of sadness, for example, could be the result of bad news, but it could also be caused by a predisposition to feeling sad resulting from childhood trauma or even just the bacteria in our gut.

Recognising true emotions can help us to intervene in the space between feelings and actions – knowing your emotions is the first step to being in control of them, breaking negative thought patterns. Understanding our own emotions and thinking patterns can also help us more easily empathise with others.

Self-awareness also allows us to make better decisions. In one study, students who scored higher on ‘metacognitive awareness’ – the ability to reflect on personal thoughts, feelings, attitudes and beliefs – tended to make more effective decisions when it came to playing a computer game in which they had to diagnose and treat virtual patients in order to cure them. The authors argued that this was because they could set well defined goals and make strategic actions.

Getting to know yourself

So how can we learn how we feel? People can have different ways of thinking about themselves. We can think about our history, and how past experiences have made us who we are. But we can also brood about negative scenarios in the past or future. Some of these ways of thinking about ourselves are better for us than others. Unfortunately, many of us tend to ruminate and to worry. That is, we focus on our fears and shortcomings, and as a result we become anxious or depressed.

The best way to start would be talking with an insightful friend or a trained therapist. The latter is especially important in cases where a lack of self-knowledge is interfering with our mental health. Putting words to feelings and being asked follow-up questions can really help us to understand who we are. Reading about useful ways of thinking can also help us to navigate our lives better.

In addition, there are several other traditions throughout our history that have explored ways of getting to know ourselves. Both Stoic philosophy and Buddhist traditions valued self-knowledge and developed practices to nurture awareness of mental states – such as meditation.

Nowadays, mindfulness meditation has gained traction in psychology, medicine and neuroscience. Meditation and emotion regulation training can reduce negative feelings, rumination and anxiety. They also increase positive emotions, improve the ability to recognise emotions in others, and protect us from social stress. Therapies that integrate mindfulness have been shown to be reliable in helping to improve mental health, specifically the outcome of depression, stress and anxiety.

By just sitting for a little while and watching our thoughts and feelings from a distance, as if we are sitting by the side of the road and watching cars go by, we can get to know ourselves better. This helps us to practise the skill of not thinking about the past or future, and we can be in the present a little bit more. We can learn to recognise the feelings that certain events and emotions trigger in us at the moment, and to create a space in which we can decide how to act (as some responses are more constructive than others).

Imagine, for example, that you have plans to go for a bike ride with a friend tomorrow and you're very much looking forward to this. In the morning, your friend cancels. Later in the day, a colleague asks you for help with a problem, and you feel annoyed and snap at them – telling them you don't have time for it.

Maybe you felt annoyed with the colleague, but the real reason was that you felt disappointed with your friend, and you now feel that you may not be as important to them as they are to you. If we're more self-aware, we're more likely to have the chance to pause and realise why we're feeling the way we're feeling. Rather than taking it out on our colleague, we can then realise that we are overreacting or identify whether there are any problems in our relationship with our friend.

It is fascinating that almost 2,500 years after the construction of the temple of Apollo, the quest to know ourselves better is still equally important.

by Niia Nilolova, University of Strathclyde

Learning gives knowledge,

knowledge gives confidence,

confidence gives character,

and character creates a

person.

A little about the author

Born in London in 1957.

Brought up on soggy vegetables, alcohol and cigarettes from a very early age, and on marijuana, coke, mushrooms, ecstasy tablets, firm vegetables etc. A little later.

Was shot at three times (once accidentally), and

imprisoned on a felony charge (Grand Auto Theft) in Dade County Jail (in Miami) at the age of twenty-five.

Been married three times, has two beautiful daughters, one wonderful grandson, and a partridge in a pear tree! (Maybe one Day)

Has Been, Oh know (Not A Has been!) Busboy, Waiter, Taxi Driver, Estate agent (sorry) mortgage broker, worked in pyramid sales in and around Liberty City and Carol City.

Worked with Social Services (Drugs and Alcohol Abuse).
Gained Degrees/Diplomas in the UK, in Psychology, Sociology, CBT and NLP.

Half-heartedly believed he was a psychotherapist, had a Space in Harley Street, but decided not to practise ('couldn't work out his own psyche, let alone others')

Now lives a sedate life on the Isle of Wight, contemplating life's strange and wonderful ways, reading and writing, trying to produce something beautiful, and says:

'There comes a time and a place for everything. The anecdotes and sayings in this book will change your life (for the better) if you regard them in truth.'

Acknowledgements.

* Special thanks to Margaret Foreman, for putting up with me every week.

1, Many Thanks To, Toni Turner, Author of (A Beginner's Guide to Short-Term Trading)

2, Many Thanks To, Charlie Finn, http://www.poetrybycharlescfinn.com

3, Much appreciated, Julivs Probst (Lund University)

4, Inspirational I wish I met you. Abraham Maslow. (The Right to be Human)

5, Wonderful words: William Hutchison Murray. (Until one is committed..)

6, Evolve your brain: (Always trying Joe) Many thanks, Written by Dr Joe Dispenza

7, The marvellous and mysterious Robert W. Service: A Rolling Stone, etc (Distant cousin)

8, Phyllis McCormack, "Crabbit Old Woman" (Beautiful Words)

9, Terry Kettering (The elephant in the room)

10, Many Thanks to Alison stone. Lancaster university.

11, Great article Niia Nilova, University of Strathclyde.

12, Merl Storr. For a thoroughly good job, Proofreading - copy-editing, copywriting.

14, Last but not least, my family for having the patience to put up with me every day.

Sorry if I've missed anyone else, my brain can only take so much
PS, mum, dad, the dogs, you get the drift!

Practice any art
No matter how well or badly
Not to get money or fame
But to experience becoming to find out what's inside YOU,
To make your soul grow.
Buy art from a living artist.

The dead ones don't need the money.

Hope you have enjoyed this book, please keep reminding not only your goodself, but others of these sayings, that will make inroads into your psyche and make one grateful for being here on this crazy planet.